Carolann Kelleher

The KING'S *Daughter*

Ark House Press
PO Box 1722, Port Orchard, WA 98366 USA
PO Box 1321, Mona Vale NSW 1660 Australia
PO Box 318 334, West Harbour, Auckland 0661 New Zealand
arkhousepress.com

Cataloguing in Publication Data:
Title: The King's Daughter
ISBN: 978-0-6485077-8-9 (pbk.)
Subjects: Biography, Christian
Other Authors/Contributors: Kelleher, Carolann

Design and layout by initiateagency.com

"I know it is difficult to believe in your own courage or fortitude when everything inside of you feels weak and shattered. But do not believe what you feel. You will not be easily broken."

—— Rachel L. Schade

I dedicate this book to my granddaughter Caitlyn, who always encouraged me and loved me unconditionally, and to my four year-old grandson, who knows nothing else but to love me. I also want to thank both my daughter in-laws, Heather and Lynda, for their support and comfort when I was in need. And to my son Leam: I thank you for never doubting me and all the encouragement you gave to me. And my son Simon, who has never given up on me.

My biggest thank you is to the King of Kings, who took me out of the mud, the mire and the clay and stood me on the solid rock and now He has made me His daughter, The King's Daughter. Thank you Father.

Contents

"Onward, and up, and up again, until the impossible was achieved, all barriers were broken, all pains conquered, all abilities possessed. Until all was lightning and no darkness left."

—— Gordon R. Dickson

Chapter 1.

ℳ child was born

It was a cold winter's night in the heart of London England. It was November 1945. World War II had just come to an end, but the people in London were not totally convinced it was over, and so there still lay in their hearts tension, fear, apprehension and oppression, which caused many dysfunctional relationships and marriages.

In fact, the government of the day encouraged the people to take up smoking and drinking alcohol excessively to help calm their nerves. But it did more than that: people became addictive to these substances. In the end, some people would do anything to get their fix, even to the point where their children were put in harm's way. The government in London of that day thought they were helping the people, but really they were setting up families to fail, and to fail miserably, and the children were the ones that suffered.

A young woman lay in her bed about to give birth to a baby; one she did not want, one she tried to abort, but failed. The father was not present. He too did not want another child and so he was in the local pub drinking. in fact, he was now so drunk he did not know who or what was going on. This was such a terrible time for all the family, but especially for the unwanted child.

The child was born a little girl. She was born into a very dysfunctional family, addicted to alcohol and cigarettes and who did not want her. Her parents did not want her, nor cared about her needs, and all the money went on their wants. There was very little left for family food and clothing.

This little girl had dark hair and very dark eyes. She was a sad little girl she was unloved and unwanted. She was exceptionally thin and her clothes would hang on her skinny, unnourished body, and people would laugh at her. Even her brothers called her names because of her ugly looks and she felt it. At school, the other children called her "Poppy's girlfriend Olive Oil." She was ugly from outside in and she felt it.

No one loved her, no one cared for her. She was all alone and outcast from her family. To them, she was an embarrassment because in their eyes, she was ugly, unwanted and a girl.

If only this little girl knew that to her Father in Heaven, she was the most beautiful girl in the world, the daughter of the King.

This young girl we will call Mary. She had a brother thirteen months older than her, and at the age of five years, her mother told her she was an unwanted pregnancy. In fact, her mother told her in detail that she tried to abort her with a knitting needle while she lay in a very hot bath when she was three months' pregnant, and every opportunity from that day forward, her mother would tell her the story of how she did not want Mary and tried to get rid of her.

As Mary grew, her mother would make fun of her because of her skinny body and her not-so-nice looks. Clothes were always seconds and hand-me-downs. They never fitted her properly; they were always too big.

One day, Mary wanted to wear a spotted green and white dress that had been given to her from a neighbour. She was about twelve years old and was at the age where girls start to think about nice clothes. Now Mary thought it was a lovely dress, but it did not fit her properly. The straps would fall off her skinny, bony shoulders all the time and her mother would laugh at her, saying how ugly she was.

This same day, Mary was in the garden. She wanted to grow her hair and so she tried to put it in a ponytail. it was far too short, but Mary insisted on wearing it in a ponytail, but her mother laughed and her brothers laughed so much the neighbour came out to see what was happening. Mary's mother made a joke about Mary and how stupid she looked and how ugly she was, then all the people were laughing at her and she began to cry. She ran into the house and locked herself in the bedroom, where she cried and cried and cried.

How humiliated she felt, how ugly she felt, how unloved she felt, and how unwanted she felt. She just wanted to die. This pain went on in Mary's heart for a very long time and even as a grown woman, her mother made fun of Mary, saying, "Remember that green spotted dress and how you put your hair in a ponytail? You look so stupid," and she started to laugh once again. Was this pain ever going to stop? Was this pain ever going to go away? Why did her mother hate her so? Why did she ridicule her to the point that Mary wanted to die?

PSALM 139:13, "FOR YOU FORMED MY INWARD PARTS, YOU COVERED ME IN MY MOTHER WOMB."

If only Mary knew that then, the pain might have stopped. God the Father protected this little girl from the snares of the devil and from the destruction that her mother tried to do. Thank you God.

"Sometimes it's not about trying to fix something that's broken. Sometimes it's about starting again and building something new. Something better"

— Leisa Rayven

Chapter 2.

A vision of hope

B y now, Mary was already a damaged child. She was always in the wrong. Whatever she did, her mother would treat her like a servant, and at school, Mary was unable to speak, and so the nuns told her parents that she was a moron, or at least mentally handicapped. She was not allowed to attend class or learn anything.

Mary would clean the church, polish the silver, and make morning and afternoon tea for the nuns at the school, instead of doing schoolwork. The only thing Mary learnt to do was to pray, but to whom she should pray she did not know. She was confused, so she would pray to the saints, the mother of Jesus and to anyone else she was instructed to pray to, but rarely to God or Jesus, as the nuns told her she was not good enough to talk to God or say the name of Jesus. She was a bad girl, and only good girls could talk to God.

Mary was in church one Friday. She was almost seven years old. Each Friday, the nuns took all the school children to church for a special service. Mary knelt next to the nun. She looked up to heaven and said in her heart, "IF THERE IS A GOD THEN SHOW ME AND MAKE ME FAINT."

Well, guess what? Mary fainted and she woke up on the steps of the church, with the nuns telling her that only girls with sin in their hearts faint in church. But Mary knew it was not true. To Mary, it was a vision of hope. She now knew that there was a God, but she still felt that she was not good enough to talk to Him. But Mary had a hope: a hope of something better; that one day someone would love her.

But would anyone ever show Mary mercy, compassion friendship and even love? The nuns said she was bad, and so she must be bad, and how could anyone love a bad girl?

> MATTHEW 19: 147 JESUS SAID, "LET THE LITTLE
> CHILDREN COME UNTO ME AND DO NOT FORBID THEM
> FOR OF SUCH IS THE KINGDOM OF HEAVEN."

But the nuns told Mary she was bad through and through. They engraved it into her heart that she was such a bad girl and always would be bad. Everything in Mary seemed to be bad. From that moment on, Mary thought all the bad things that happened to her was her fault. But Mary did know that there was a God, and over the years, she learnt that God did love her. God loved Mary so much He sent His son Jesus to die for her.

But it took many years for Mary to truly comprehend this, and so she had to go through years and years of being unloved, unwanted, dropped, sexually abused and physically beaten until she was a damaged, broken, unloved and rejected woman. And she felt it... nothing would change this feeling of being unloved.

JOHN 3:16 "FOR GOD SO LOVED THE WORLD THAT HE GAVE HIS ONLY BEGOTTEN SON, THAT WHOEVER BELIEVES IN HIM SHOULD NOT PERISH BUT HAVE EVERLASTING LIFE."

At age seven, another brother was born and that made Mary's life even harder. Mary had to look after the baby while her mother and father smoked and drank until they were drunk, and no money was left for food again and again. But somehow, there was always food and clothing and affection for her brothers by her parents, but none for her. Mary's mother would say each day, "Why can't you be like your brothers? Look how good they are."

When her parents drank, they got agitated and angry, but they only took it out on Mary. Oh, how Mary hated those days. She even wondered if she hated her brothers because they were boys and they were favoured by her parents.

Mary's grandmother, who she called nanny Ann, was a lifesaver. Nanny would give Mary crusts of bread that tasted like roast dinner, with Yorkshire pudding and gravy, whenever nanny could. Mary loved to visit nanny. if nothing else, nanny gave her milk to drink and some food and she was allowed to sit in front of the fire to warm herself. Mary just loved those times. If only they were more often.

When Mary was 16 years old, nanny told Mary that her father had forced himself upon her when her mother was pregnant with Mary. Nanny was crying and Mary consoled her, but said nothing.

Another person in Mary's life was her granddad, Harry. He was very nice to Mary and tried to protect her. But again, Mary's father got drunk, beat up grandad Harry, and pushed him down the stairs. Mary saw this and tried to help grandad Harry, as he was hurt, but her father then took his belt to Mary until her back bled.

Grandad Harry died when Mary was 12 years-old and nanny Ann died when Mary was 25 years-old. Mary had lost her only true friends.

Grandad Harry was a coachman to a Lord and Lady and one day, grandad took Mary to Buckingham Palace to see the changing of the guards. She was just eight years-old. Then Mary had a great surprise: grandad knew one of the guards and they were taken to the stables to see the horses in the palace grounds. It was so exciting that Mary never forgot that day. It was the best day of her childhood. That day, she was a little girl being treated by her grandad. What a wonderful time that was. She never forgot the love and kindness that her grandad gave her.

Another time, Mary was taken by her parents to Trafalgar Square in the heart of London. This was to be a special day, but it turned out to be a terrible one. Trafalgar Square is known for the amount of pigeons that would gather there, waiting patiently to be fed by the tourists. Little did Mary know this; she was extremely frightened of birds.

Her parents took her into the middle of the Square and she was told to stay there. Her parents disappeared, leaving her in the midst of hundreds of birds. They literally came from nowhere and landed on Mary head, shoulders, arms... in fact anywhere they could. Well, Mary screamed and started to run and run and run, and then she stopped and saw her parents and brothers laughing at her. Devastated, Mary ran and ran and ran until she was lost.

She was eventually found by the police and brought back to her parents, where she was verbally abused. When they eventually went home, Mary was beaten because of her fear of birds. How she just wanted to die. Why couldn't they just love her and care for her? Life was unbearable and she was very lonely. All she wanted was to be loved, but love was nowhere to be found.

"If you are faced with a mountain,
you have several options.

You can climb it and cross to the other side.

You can go around it.

You can dig under it.

You can fly over it.

You can blow it up.

You can ignore it and pretend it's not there.

You can turn around and go
back the way you came.

Or you can stay on the mountain
and make it your home."

—— Vera Nazarian,

Chapter 3.

The black years

Let us go back a few years. When Mary was only three years-old, her father commenced to abuse her. He would take her into the shed and do things she did not like. But her father told her that is what fathers do, and she had to like it. She had to believe it, because her father said it, and everyone knows fathers don't lie. You never challenge or disagree with your father. If you did, watch out. Violence and anger was on the way.

Mary was confused because she did not like what her father was doing to her. it made her cry, but her father said if she cried, he would hurt her more. He then said to Mary, "This is our secret and if you keep this secret, then I will give you some sweets." (as they were called then. Now we call them lollies.) Well, Mary only understood that if she did not cry, she would get some sweets and that was her treat. Remember, when this started, Mary was only three years-old; just a baby. How could anyone want to hurt an innocent baby?

There was no love from Mary's mother or her father, but her father told Mary on many occasions while he was hurting her that he loved her, and she tried to believe it. So to Mary, she thought that any form of hurt or abuse was love; that the person loved her. How wrong can you be? How wrong Mary was. Her mother showed nothing but dislike to Mary, and every one knew it –especially Mary – but she did not want to believe it.

When Mary was coming on to eight years-old, she went to the local park with her older brother. The park was called Ally Pally Park, and on occasions they were allowed to go and Mary's brother was supposed to look after her. He was a year older than Mary. This particular day, a man came up to Mary and her brother and asked if they would help him find his dog that had run into the bushes. Mary's brother said yes, and so Mary followed.

The man took them into the bushes and pretended to look for the dog and called out the dog's name. The man started to touch Mary in places she did not want. She tried to run away, but he held on to her and would not let her go. He offered her lollies and she stopped struggling and Mary looked around for her brother and saw him running away. Mary's brother was supposed to look after her, and there he was, running away, leaving her to be hurt once again. Mary was left again, rejected again by her brother, and her heart just sank.

Mary tried to follow her brother, but the man would not let her go. The man forced Mary onto the ground. Oh how heavy he was she could not breath. She tried to scream, but nothing came out of her mouth. Mary started to cry, but there was no noise. Instead, a waterfall came out of her eyes.

The man was hurting her and everything went blank. Then she heard a voice: "What are you doing to the girl?" The man got up and ran away. Mary's clothes were torn. She was shaken; she also was frightened as to what her mother and father would say. She said nothing; she just lay there. Then she heard a lady's voice: "Come on dear, let's get you home."

Home? What was going to happen at home? What was going to be her punishment? She would soon find out. Mary's mother shouted at her for tearing her clothes and then for going with the man. Mary's brother told their parents that Mary wanted to stay with the man because he gave her sweets. Mary was told that she was a bad girl and that she always would be a bad girl. "Why can't you be like your brothers?" her mother would shout.

Again, it was Mary's fault, what ever went wrong? It was always her fault. Oh, how she wanted it all to stop, how she wanted peace in her life. But no peace ever came for this little girl. Why couldn't her brother just say the truth: that he ran away and left her there to be attacked? He did not care about his sister; he only cared about himself. His thoughts were self-preservation not about a defenceless little girl, his little sister.

Mary cried and cried. Oh, what was happening to her and why? "It's because I'm bad," she thought. "Why can't I be good? I will always be bad. The nuns told me so and my parents told me so. But I don't want to be bad. I want to be good, nice and be loved. When will all the pain stop?" These were Mary's thoughts day after day. When will the pain stop?

Later, her father got her on her own and told her that only he was to touch Mary in that way because he loved her. Mary smiled, hoping that he was not going to hurt her, and thank God he did not hurt her for a few weeks.

PROVERBS 3: 5 "TRUST IN THE LORD WITH ALL YOUR
HEART AND LEAN NOT ON YOUR OWN UNDERSTANDING"

Well, by the age of eight years-old, the time in the shed with her father was every week when her mother went out shopping, and for two to three hours at a time. She hated this time, but loved the sweets. It was a treat she received for keeping the secret. Later in life, Mary became very ashamed of her actions. She felt guilty because she did not expose what was going on, what the monster was doing to her and other girls, but the monster was her father. Mary always blamed herself because she was bad, but what about her father, the monster? Was he bad, or was it all Mary's fault?

Mary always wanted to say, 'Stop, leave me alone," but when she did try, her father then hurt her more, so Mary just took whatever he did and waited for the sweets. They were lovely and they were hers and she did not have to share then with her brothers. Oh, how she loved the sweets, but she hated the secret. She hated what he did.

Time after time, Mary would try to hide from her father. She would visit nextdoor neighbours and play with their children, but her father would find her and bring her back, back to brutal abuse that no child should have to endure even once in their lives, let alone every week.

On these abusive occasions, Mary would drift into another world so that she could not feel the hurt. This little girl was abused and broken. Would she ever be able to have a normal life? Would she ever have a normal relationship with anyone? Would anyone ever love her, cherish her, respect her, or would her life be nothing but abuse?

These abusive and hurtful sessions: would they keep going on forever? Would they ever stop? Mary would ask herself these questions time after time. One night when Mary was asleep, her father came into her room and tried to wake her, but she pretended to still be asleep. He got into her bed and Mary started to pray in her heart: "Please God, make him go away."

Mary's father started to do things to her. She lay very quiet, still pretending to be asleep. Then Mary heard her mother's voice. "Jack, Jack," in a harsh voice she said. "Leave her alone come back to our bed," and so he did.

MARY'S PRAYER "THANK YOU GOD FOR SAVING ME FROM ANOTHER NIGHT OF FEAR AND HURT."

Mary started to think that maybe God liked her because He stopped the abuse for at least one time.

When Mary was about 10 years-old, she had three school friends: Barbara, Freda and Yvonne. One Saturday they had come to play with Mary at her home. This was the first and the last time Mary had friends come to play. When Mary's mother went shopping, she thought that her time in the shed with her father would not happen, but it did.

Mary so wanted it to not happen. She even pleaded with her father, asking if they could go to the park and play and not in the shed. But with no avail, her father had his own way. He pretended to be nice to Mary and her friends, but Mary knew what was going to happen, and she so did not want it. In fact, she wanted to die.

Her father took all the girls into the shed and began to abuse them. Mary cried in her heart, "No, no, no, please no," but it still happened. Mary's friends began to cry, and so her father told them to put their clothes on and go home, and if they told anyone, he would come and hurt them again. Mary's friends never came to the house again. In fact, they did not even play with her at school ever again. Once again, Mary was dropped and rejected, this time by her school friends. Now the school friends were no more her friends. She was alone.

She was now rejected, unloved, dropped, abandoned and very ashamed. She had no friends to play with, no one to talk to, no one to laugh with or cry with. Mary became even more of a loner. She withdrew from every one. Even the teachers at her primary school verbally abused her, saying how ugly she was. But Mary said nothing because she felt bad and dirty and unloved, unwanted. She felt rejected by everyone. Nobody liked her or loved her.

But still, God never left Mary. He never forgot her. He was always with her. He protected her; He had a plan for Mary's life, a plan that would come to fruition.

JEREMIAH 15: 21 "FOR I AM WITH YOU TO SAVE YOU AND DELIVER YOU SAYS THE LORD. I WILL DELIVER YOU FROM THE HAND OF THE

WICKED AND I WILL REDEEM YOU FROM THE GRIP OF THE TERRIBLE".

When Mary's three friends left, Mary's father continued to hurt her repeatedly until her mother came home. If Mary cried, she would get beaten with the buckle part of the belt. These beatings only happened a few times because Mary learnt to cry in her heart and not out loud. It was then that Mary found a way to overcome the hurt, a way to block the pain in her heart.

Mary would, in her mind, fly above the abuse and she could see the abuse and not feel it. Many years later, Mary knew that it was God who had lifted her above the hurt and saved her from hell.

PSALM 91: 15 – 15 "BECAUSE SHE HAS SET HER LOVE UPON ME I WILL DELIVER HER, I WILL SET HER ON HIGH BECAUSE SHE HAS KNOWN MY NAME, SHE SHALL CALL UPON ME AND I WILL ANSWER HER. I WILL BE WITH HER IN TIMES OF TROUBLE, I WILL DELIVER HER AND HONOUR HER WITH LONG LIFE, I WILL SATISFY HER AND SHOW HER MY SALVATION." PRAISE THE LORD

"Some days are sweetened with pure, but fleeting joy. Just keep keeping on.

Some days consist of a kind of sorrow that tries to break you. Just keep keeping on.

Some days are filled with bright, warm light that clearly shows the path to follow. Just keep keeping on.

Some days are filled with calm and peace. Just keep keeping on.

Some days are filled with a violent commotion

that does its best to disrupt our innermost harmony. Just keep keeping on.

Some days we must just take a rest, until we can once again, keep keeping on.

Some days are filled with hope and faith and the recognition of a journey we wouldn't trade for anything. And so we keep keeping on."

— Connie Kerbs

Chapter 4.

Decisions, decisions, which one shall I make?

As the years went by, Mary was completely damaged. She felt dropped, hurt, broken, confused, angry and of no use to anyone, as well as being undesirable to any decent man. She felt so unloved and rejected, so unwanted, so dirty. She felt that she was a gutter person and not good enough to even breathe fresh air. She wanted to die, but something made her go on and on.

Mary had watched her grandfather kill a chicken. She was amazed how easy it was. Now the chicken was not screeching anymore. It was dead. No pain anymore, and she thought, "How could I kill myself? Grandad Harry just took a knife and cut the throat of the chicken."

It seemed so simple. Could she do this to herself? This was in Mary's thoughts on many occasions in her young life and also well into adulthood.

Mary was defeated. She was at the bottom of life, she knew no way out or up. She wanted out but how. She did no know. There must be more to life Mary cried to herself. I just want it all to stop, with the knife she could stop it, did she have the courage to use the knife. Mary felt a failure she could not end it all and she could not keep going. What was her fate, could she just lay down and die.

Later in life Mary knew it was God who gave her the strength to go on and on, to not end it all, it was His strength, His grace, His love that gave her the strength to endure many years of abuse. And Mary would for the rest of her life say thankyou to Jesus for saving her.

JERIMIAH 16: 19 "OH LORD MY STRENGTH AND MY FORTRESS, MY REFUGE IN THE DAY OF AFFLICTION. PSALM 29: 11 "THE LORD WILL GIVE STRENGTH TO HIS PEOPLE".

Praise God He did give Mary all the strength she needed, without Him Mary would never survive but He had great plans for Mary, oh how He loved her.

But Mary kept remembering what the nun had told her, she was a bad girl and that only girls with sin in their hearts faint in church, so all that Mary's father did to her she thought it was her fault. Even though her father said he loved her and when you love someone this is what you do. It was Marys fault she thought, she was bad, she brought it upon herself, her guilt was eating her mind away.

Later Mary thought how wrong he was, in fact he was a monster looking for his own satisfaction, not caring for a little defenceless girl. This father destroyed this little girl life. Mary hated him, this monster she had to call father. Why couldn't she have a loving family, one who wanted her, loved her, but it was no good dreaming it would never happen. No one would ever love me she thought, no one would ever care about me, I am not worthy of any thing good.

Mary was deceived and confused, she tried to believe her father when he said he loved her but she knew it was not true, but she had to believe it, her father said so. She now thought that if you are being abused that means you are being loved. Oh, how wrong she was. Would Mary ever find the truth about love. Would she ever feel loved, would anyone ever want to love her?

Why did this happen to her, she was just a little girl Mary would often ask herself. Later in Mary's life she would ask why oh why, But God knew what was happening and he protected her over and over again. Jesus loved her but she did not know it, but one day she would know, one day she would find out the truth. Jesus is love.

In Matthew 19: 147 Jesus said "let the little children come unto Me and do not forbid them for of such is the kingdom of heaven.

But as time went on and Mary was coming on for 18 years, she knew what her father was doing was wrong and she hated it, she did not want to be hurt any more but she was frightened of her father, she did not know how to stop him. This monster frightened her she tried to get away, but her father would not let her.

He threatened her saying, if you try to go away, I will find you and kill. At one time Mary thought that this was the best way out, to be killed, to die and not to be hurt ever again. But for some reason she kept living, she did not give up the fight to stay alive.

So, at the age of 18 years Mary stood up to her father and said NO and pushed him away, she shouted don't touch me ever again. That's when he hit her broke her nose, fractured her cheek and knocked her out and beat her so badly and left her in a pool of blood.

When Mary came too, she got up and ran out of the house, she ended up in hospital, but she never went back to the home again. The police came to see Mary in the hospital and said they do not get involved in domestic issues. Oh, how times have changed, and the police these days would have arrested the father and put in jail for life. But in those days a father and mother could do what they wanted with their child and Mary's parents did just that.

They, Marys parents stole her childhood, they purposefully and selfishly took it away from her, it was all about their wants and their needs their selfish satisfaction and devious ways. Their favourite word was, me, me, me, me, and take, take and take they never knew how to give just take. They were very dysfunctional and maybe the war had something to do with that, maybe the war changed people into monsters, one day we might find that out.

Parents are supposed to love their children but Marys parents hated her, why she did not know, she only thought it was because she was bad, ugly and unwanted. But one day Mary would know the truth.

After being released from hospital Mary had nowhere to go, she had nowhere to lay her head, she went to her grandmothers and asked if she could stay but she said no, Mary went to her aunt and she said no. They told her she was a bad girl and should go home and stop being bad and stop making trouble for the family.

These relatives either did not believe her or they did not want to. But Mary knew she could never go back to that abuse ever again.

It was getting late, getting dark she had only the cloths on her back. Mary was feeling very frightened, she felt rejected, unloved, dirty, used and ugly. Mary was at her wits end. She did not know where to turn to for help (it was 1963). Not like today 2019 when there are so many people to help a young girl who is being repeatedly abused.

Where do I go, she thought, what do I do she mouthed out loud as tears ran down her face? There was no where to go, not like today where there are hostels to stay in. There was nowhere for Mary to stay she had to make things happen, her thoughts were, do I stay alive or should I just lay down and die. Which was the better of two evils, to die or not to die that was the question.

That night she slept on a bench in the park, then at the train station, she also found a toilet in a park where she could lock herself in and try to sleep sitting up. Mary went night after night for two weeks then she said to herself I must find a place to stay, she had not had a bath for some time, she was hungry, the little money she had was gone. What was she to do, who would take care of her, who would give her a roof over her head?

There was one person she knew that liked her his name was Bill, and so she went to his house and he accepted her, and they were married within a few months.

"Sometimes there's a fire in your
life and you ask God,

"Lord, let me go around the fire."
And God says, "No."

Then you ask, "Lord, then let me go over the fire."

And God says, "No." Then you ask,

"Well Lord, please let me go under the fire."

And God says, "No. Go through
the fire and I'll be with you."

—— Lydia Thornton

Chapter 5.

The silver lining or was it.

Mary thought this was the silver lining that people talked about that never again would she be abused, hit or punished again. But she was wrong within a short time the anger commenced and the bruises started to show and Mary would say to other people, Oh I fell against the door or something like that.

But Mary's husband would hit her, and abuse her, he was angry at her. But it was not always his fault, Mary was disturbed, she was heading for a mental breakdown. Time after time Mary would run away and then came back not knowing where she had been. She was not aware of what she was doing or where she went to, to Mary it was a black hole in her life.

This was not her husband's fault, Mary did not know or understand her actions or her thought pattern. Mary would lock herself into the bathroom for hours, lay in the bath and sink beneath the water and try not to come up for air, but she always came up for air.

Mary really want to die, life was too hard for her. She would hide under the bed, lock Bill out of the house, Mary was on the verge of a breakdown and with in the year she had one.

Mary went into hospital and just wanted to die, she felt so unloved, unwanted, rejected, she hated herself and all the world. While she was in hospital, they gave her electric shock treatment and by Gods grace after 3 months became well again never to go down that track again. Praise God.

HEBREWS 13:5A "I WILL NEVER LEAVE YOU OR FORSAKE YOU."

By now Mary was a very broken woman she had 2 children and after 11 years of being unloved she ran away and took the children with her. Well thats not quite true, Mary did run away but the circumstances were a little different, Mary found once again she was pregnant and when she told her husband he said "I will stay until the baby is born and then I am leaving as I have fallen in love with someone else." And that is what he did. When the baby was born, Mary had to leave the house with her 3 children, one only a few weeks old to find accommodation that she could afford.

Mary once again was homeless, rejected, unloved, not wanted tossed aside like a piece of rubbish. All Mary ever wanted was to be loved and cherished. But love never came. Mary went to a woman's refuge with her children this was a big mistake as she was attacked and abused physically and mentally by the staff and other residences, she had to get out of there.

Mary's mind was so confused, what life had she brought on her children, she wanted to give them love and stability, but it always went bad. If only Mary had realized that it was her bad choices in life that caused her instability, her pain, her anguish and her rejection. But she knew nothing else all she remembered was what the nuns had told her, she was bad and would always be bad. She was dirty and would always be dirty, she was rejected and would always be rejected, she was unloved and would always be unloved. Who would want such a dirty ugly woman, no one she thought.

OH, how Mary wanted out once again of the situation, but something urged her to keep going, to make a better life for her children. And that is what she did.

A person, a man, he was an acquaintance of Marys offered her to share his house and so Mary took that offer up, but that was another mistake, another bad decision and other bad choice.

Let me explain, the reasons Mary made many bad choices was because she was desperate and when anyone is so desperate and they don't know Jesus they cling on to anything that might look like it could be good. This time it was terrible for Mary.

Now Mary had nowhere to go she had to find a roof over her children's head, get some food into their tummies help them to feel loved even if she was not loved she vowed that she would show love to them and make sure they were never without ever again. Mary vowed she would sacrifice all for her children and that is what she did. Mary gave away her life so that her children would have life and life abundantly.

Mary made sure that her children attended private schools, dance lessons, golf lessons, music lessons. You see Mary found herself a good job as an estimator (little did she know that God gave her the job) and she gave her children all that she never had including much love. But Mary still felt unloved, rejected, not wanted by her family and by society.

THAT'S WHAT JESUS SAID IN JOHN 10:10 "I HAVE COME THAT THEY MAY HAVE LIFE AND THAT THEY MAY HAVE IT MORE ABUNDANTLY."

If only Mary knew that Jesus loved her and wanted only good for her and her children, He wanted to give her life and life abundantly.

Mary was a devoted mother, it was her choice to put her children first and herself last. But Mary had to get away from this house as the acquaintance tried to abuse her and take advantage of her. And so again Mary was homeless with 3 children, it happened time after time, again and again.

Now let me stop here about Mary and look at the story of the woman at the well. This is a true story from the bible.

"At the moment when the road looks the harshest, and you think you cannot continue on that is when you relearn your first mode of transportation; you crawl. You dig your fingers into the dirt, and propel yourself forward with your toes, but you never give up. You've gotta learn to bend with the sway. You never know what is around the next curve."

—— Sai Marie Johnson

Chapter 6.

The woman at the well

MATTHEW 25: 31 "WHEN THE SON OF MAN IN HIS GLORY AND ALL HIS ANGELS WITH HIM, THEN HE WILL SIT ON THE THRONE OF HIS GLORY. ALL THE NATIONS WILL BE GATHERED BEFORE HIM AND HE WILL SEPARATE THEM FROM ONE ANOTHER AS A SHEPHERD SEPARATES HIS SHEEP FROM THE GOATS. AND HE WILL CAUSE THE SHEEP TO STAND AT HIS RIGHT HAND BUT THE GOATS AT HIS LEFT. THEN THE KING WILL SAY TO THOSE AT HIS RIGHT HAND, COME YOU BLESSED OF MY FATHER INHERIT THE KINGDOM PREPARED FOR YOU FROM THE FOUNDATION OF THE WORLD."

Let me tell you about the Samarian woman at the well. She told her village people about Jesus and many believed and gave their hearts to Jesus.

This lady was an outcast. She had been married five times and was living with another man, but Jesus loved her and gave her a job to do for Him.

He filled her up to overflowing and she preached the gospel of Jesus's love.

Jesus forgave her because it was not her fault and she repented. She was a victim of many angry men, but this woman was so very sorry for all her mistakes, her bad choices. She wanted to live for Him and Him alone. (That reminds me of the story of Mary)

You know, I have thought long and hard about this woman at the well: how she must have felt and what was her reasoning for her lifestyle and her life choices. Did she have a choice? I don't think so. Well, at that time she thought she had no choice, but time would tell.

Let me give you a scenario that I believe could be the reasons why this Samarian woman lived, or choose to live, her lifestyle.

Now the Samarian woman married a man, a man she was either told to marry, or was sold to marry. She had no choice in the matter. She would have been around the age of 15 years. Women at this time had little or no say in their lives. Women were the possession of men; women were treasured by some men, but were beaten and controlled by other men.

This Samaritan woman married, but things did not work out for her in this marriage. Maybe the husband grew tired of her, or she did not give birth to a boy. Maybe her housekeeping skills were not the best, or maybe her husband was abusive or violent and out of control. And then may be this lady had an illness such as Chronic Fatigue Syndrome, or another depilating illness that no one could cure.

Whatever the problem, her husband did not care, but he took steps to divorce her and she was forced to leave the house and home. She was beaten and rejected, unloved and had nowhere to go. In those days, only a man could divorce his wife and a woman could not leave the marital home, unless the husband divorced her. He was her life source; there was no social security and no other way to get food or shelter but to be with a man. Remember, in those days, the man had control of all females within his household.

So, this Samaritan woman had to leave the household.

Yes, she was rejected, and she felt it. She was unloved and she felt it. Where could she go? Who would look after her? How could she get food? She was desperate; she was depressed. What was her fate now?

All these thoughts would have probably gone through her mind. The only thing she could do was to marry another man so that he could provide for her. This time she would try harder. She would show him more love, do the things he wanted and hopefully she would bare him a son. What plans she had, she was so determined to make this marriage a success.

But sadly, after a short time, she realised she had married the same sort of man and not far down the track her husband took steps to devoice her. Was he violent, abusive? We don't know, we can only just imagine.

Now this lady was devastated. She wanted to be loved and cherished she wanted to be wanted for who she was, and now she once again was rejected. She would have gone through the same thoughts and more as she did before.

Yes, she was rejected again, and she felt it. She was unloved once again and she felt it. Where could she go? Who would look after her? How could she get food? Where would she lay her head? Why couldn't she be loved and wanted? What was she doing wrong? She was desperate, she was depressed. What was her fate now?

Again, and again this very sad and lonely woman went through this process: through broken hearts, through beatings. Some almost killed her. She went through loneliness, through rejection until she had been married five times and the same story with each husband, and the fifth one took steps to divorce her.

By this time the Samaritan woman had hardened her heart. She was totally rejected and unloved and she felt it.

This time she was not going to allow a man to rule over her. She would keep the next man on his toes. She would not marry him but live with him. Then he could not divorce her. I wonder what type of man she found? Maybe a criminal, or a man who treated women with disrespect. GOD ONLY KNOWS.

At this point, I would like to ask a question: where were the husbands, the five husbands who were supposed to cherish and love her? Shouldn't they be taking some responsibility for the failed marriages?

Don't get me wrong. I'm not blaming the men, I'm not out to point the finger. I just want you to see a different picture from the one some people believe.

LOVE COVERS ALL THINGS. EPHESIANS 5: 25 SAYS "HUSBANDS LOVE YOUR WIVES JUST AS CHRIST ALSO LOVED THE CHURCH AND GAVE HIMSELF FOR HER."

Did any of these five men love her? Did they cherish her, honour her, respect her? Did they give up their life for her? I wonder if the first husband had attempted just one of these attributes, there might not have been a number two husband.

But the Samaritan woman was rejected and humiliated. She was ashamed. She had lost her confidence and her self-esteem. She wanted to hide from the other women in the village. She could not face them. The guilt was overpowering in her heart and mind. She was a broken woman. Something made her go on in life, but she did not know what.

This poor woman was hurting. Her heart was breaking, but no one could see or knew how much she was hurting. No one seemed to even care.

When the Samaritan woman came to the well that day, she came alone. She had no friends to walk and talk with. She was an outcast and classed as an immoral woman and her life choices had cost her much. She found herself isolated from normal friendships. She was a very lonely woman.

Then she met Jesus and He engaged her in conversation. She was shocked that He would talk to a woman like her. She was shocked that He even cared. She could see He wanted to befriend her and to help her. She gave her heart to him and her life changed.

This lady, the woman at the well, became the first woman evangelist to preach the gospel of Jesus Christ. She became famous because of God.

God can change our lives if we let him. All we have to do is repent and our sins are forgiven and thrown into the sea of forgetfulness. That is what happened to the woman at the well, and because of her repentance, she became famous.

"No amount of me trying to explain myself was doing any good. I didn't even know what was going on inside of me, so how could I have explained it to them?"

— Sierra D. Waters

Chapter 7.

Ashamed, unloved, unwanted.

Can you see the resemblance now in this story of the woman at the well and the story of Mary? They both were hurting, damaged, unwanted, dropped, broken and rejected by people who said they loved them.

Mary married again and again, and each time she married the same sort of man: one who would beat her, one who would control her, one who would have affairs with other woman, one who would try to kill her. The same thing happened, just like the woman at the well.

Mary was defeated, unwanted, unloved; thrown on to the rubbish heap. She was struggling to survive, but something kept her going. Something gave her strength to go on.

PHILIPPIANS 4: 13 "WE CAN DO ALL THING IN CHRIST JESUS WHO STRENGTHENS US"

If only Mary knew Jesus at that time, she might not have gone through more abuse. If only she knew that Jesus loved her more than she could ever realise, life might have been more bearable, but she didn't and so she continued to make many bad choices.

Later Mary realised that it was God who gave her the strength to continue and not to give up. It was Jesus that saved her from hell.

Then the big day came and Mary met Jesus and He changed her life. With Jesus's, help she picked herself up out of the gutter and God changed her completely.

Over the next ten years, Mary's life change. She became a disciple of Jesus Christ, just like the woman at the well. She obtained a degree in Ministry, she became a Justice of the peace, a visiting justice in the prison system and a pastor. She taught English as a second language, she was a prominent person in society and many people looked up to her. But they did not know her past and Mary did not want anyone to know. She kept the secret of her past life and no one knew it.

She was still ashamed of her past. She could not forgive herself. Mary could not forget the trauma she went through and she blamed herself for everything in her past. Even though God had thrown her past, her sins, into the sea of forgetfulness, Mary could not forget it or forgive herself. It was like a heavy chain around her neck, pulling her down and down, till she would sink beneath the water. Then the pain of shame might stop.

All this time, Mary was afraid of most males. She tried hard not to show it. She told herself that no man would ever hurt her again. Mary was determined not to make the same mistakes. She would show the world that no one was going to hurt her, no one was going to reject her, drop her, abuse her, use or neglect her in any way ever, ever again.

Mary vowed she would never forgive those people who hurt her. Little did Mary know that when you give your heart to God, then He sends His Holy Spirit to help you in many arrears, and one of them is to forgive. To forgive all persons who abuse and all persons who reject and all persons that hurt others in any way.

Mary was even able after a few years to forgive her parents, and on her father's death bed, he said, "Mary, I have always looked upon you as another woman, and I now look upon you are my daughter. Can you please forgive me?"

Well, Mary said yes. She found it so easy to forgive, as she had been forgiven so much. She knew that God had forgiven her and thrown her sins into the sea of forgetfulness, never to be looked at again.

For 20 years, Mary worked for the Commonwealth Employment Services, now known as Centrelink, and in 1996, she took a redundancy package and commenced working for her church, where she worshiped the Lord. Mary just loved her church. There she felt safe, there she could find peace. There she found true love from the senior pastor and his wife. She felt that she was in heaven, but she knew God wanted more of her. Bible College was the next step: spending five years learning God's word, His will and His ways.

Mary was the organiser of the welfare department and the outreach within her church to those girls who were abused and helped them to overcome their guilt (like all women who are abused, they feel that it is their fault and they became deeply guilty and ashamed). Mary was just a baby when all this started. How could she be guilty?

Mary started to relax more and dedicated herself to her position in the church, but she still felt guilty. God was calling Mary to step out in faith, for He had much work for her to do. But she never felt worthy. Her past was still there. She felt she could never forgive herself. Still she never told anyone about the abuse, it was still too painful.

On one occasion, when Mary was traveling from Kalgoorlie to Perth, Australia, she heard the voice of God say, "Mary, you have given me your heart. Now will you give me your life for the rest of your life?"

This was a shock to Mary. She was not prepared for this question. Her thoughts were, *what if God sends me to a place where there is no housing, no showers, no English-speaking people and she would never see her family again?* There was no answer that she could give God at that time, but every time she went to pray, the same voice and question she would hear. "Mary, will you give me your life for the rest of your life?"

Eventually Mary said, "YES, YES, YES, you can have all of me, I am yours. Thy will be done." And the Lord blessed her.

In the year 1999, around August, Mary was invited to visit a church organisation in Toowoomba in Queensland. Mary went for a few days and they offered her the position as pastor and chaplain. So, in the year 2000, she took up the position.

Mary knew God was directing her path, but it was still a very big step to take. She said to God, "I don't have money to go to Queensland, but if I am to go, You have to organise it."

The next Sunday at church, the senior pastor told the congregation that Mary had been invited to Queensland and thanked her for all the ministry she had done. Then the pastor took up an offering for her, which was a surprise, and that gave her enough money to get to Queensland and for her belongs to get there with a little left over. Praise God.

"Be of good cheer. Do not think of today's failures, but of the success that may come tomorrow. You have set yourselves a difficult task, but you will succeed if you persevere; and you will find a joy in overcoming obstacles. Remember, no effort that we make to attain something beautiful is ever lost."

—— Helen Keller

Chapter 8.

The Challenge.

The congregation Mary looked after in Toowoomba needed a lot of pastoral care, as the position was in a retirement village, a hostel, a nursing home and a hospital. So she called for some volunteers to train in pastoral care and six men, four from bible college and two who were unemployed, took up the challenge. Mary commenced this program to teach these men to become chaplains so that they would be able to give pastoral care to this large congregation and their families.

Mary became quite close to one man who seemed to be gentle and concerning of others, and so in 2002, Mary married this man. She felt that God spoke to her and said, "This is the man I want you to marry," and so she did.

To this day Mary still believed that God spoke to her to marry this man, but on her wedding night, Mary knew she had made another mistake. Anger and violence commenced, but Mary decided she would make the best of it, as she was a Christian and did not want to have another divorce.

After this first outrage of violence, the husband apologised and said it would not happen again. This was true for about three months, and then it happened again. Then he would say sorry and it would not happen for another three months.

After two years in Toowoomba, Mary was homesick and decided to return to Perth where her children and grandchild lived.

Then after a few weeks in Perth, Mary got a phone call from her son. He had cancer, so Mary had to help look after him. It was a hard time for all the family, with chemo and hospital visits, as well as long stays in hospital for her son, and Mary spent many a day helping look after her granddaughter, who was only three years old, while her son and daughter-in-law were at the hospital.

All this time, Mary's husband became jealous of the time she spent with her family. All this time, he got more and more angry, more violent, and Mary became more and more frightened, but she covered up the violence and the bruises by saying she walked into a door, or fell over, or tripped, but when people saw the bruises, they really knew what was happening. Violence was rampant in Mary's life once again.

Mary tried to hide the hurt, the violence and the abuse. She realized that her husband did not love her or cherish her, but was always angry, violent or having affairs with other women.

After 16 years, nothing had changed. In fact, it was worse. Mary kept the violence to herself for a long time, then she told her daughter-in-law and her son, as they had witnessed one or more of his anger, rage and abusive outbursts and physical abuse of Mary.

All this time, Mary was a children's pastor looking after children, making sure none of them were hurt in any way, while she herself was being damaged, dropped, hurt and abused, rejected and unloved continually. She prayed and prayed. She called out to God for the abuse to stop, to end. All Mary wanted was love. All she got was abuse.

But God was still with Mary. He was still blessing her in other ways. He was building her up for the next season He had for her.

Then there came a day when Mary was invited to plant a church in her hometown. She knew that God was speaking to her, she knew that God wanted her to plant this church to glorify Him. And she did it all for Him. It was never about her authority, her control, or her pride. It was all about God and what He wanted. Mary's prayers were always, "THY KINGDOM COME, THY WILL BE DONE." AMEN.

So Mary spoke to her husband and he promised he would stop his anger. He said once again he was sorry, but he was already planning to destroy her, as she was now a Justice of the Peace, a Visiting Justice in the prisons, a Senior Pastor, a Radio Announcer and the Director of a Kindergarten, Out of School Care and a Day-care Centre.

This husband, this man, who should have loved and cherished Mary: he just wanted to pull her down and destroy her, as he had achieved nothing in his life and was jealous of what Mary had achieved. If only he realised that it was God's plan and not Mary's plan and it was all for God's glory. THY KINGDOM, COME THY WILL BE DONE.

This man, Mary's husband, was out of control, but she could do nothing to stop him. She prayed and prayed for her marriage to get better. Mary would write in her diary, "Please God, help me. Show me how to make this marriage into what you ordained it to be," but nothing got better. It just got worse.

Time after time, when the husband was so angry, he would beat Mary. He would then say sorry, but there was no remorse or repentance. He would only say sorry. It was like water off a duck's back. He never meant it; he was never really sorry. This was his way of trying to control Mary and to pull her down.

But Mary kept praying and asking God for His will to be done. Over and over again, she would call out to God, asking how should she change, what should she do to make things better. The Lord said to Mary:-

"Each person on the earth has a freewill, they choose to go My way to heaven, or their own way to hell."

You see, Mary loved her husband and wanted only good for him and that their relationship would get better. Mary wanted to please him. She would do almost anything to keep the peace, but peace never came.

She did not want to fail again; she was prepared to do anything to keep the marriage. Mary was beside herself as her husband became more and more angry, and the violence became an everyday occurrence. Mary believed that he had a mental illness, and still to this day, believes that this is true.

He started to steal things from building sites and other places. This confirmed to Mary that he was very mentally sick, as he viewed the stealing as borrowing, but he never gave the things back. Mary even lied to protect him to cover up his affairs with other young women and even covered up the time he tried to have an affair with a home stay girl from Japan, who was only 17 years old. Mary would cover up his stealing, his abuse of other church members, and the last resort was when he was caught grooming a young girl who was blind for sex.

Mary prayed and prayed that her marriage would change for the better, but to no avail. It continued to get worse. Mary knew if she exposed her husband for who he was and what he was doing, it would end her marriage, so she tried to hang on and kept praying.

Mental illness seemed the only explanation for this man's actions and Mary was convinced of that. He locked her out of their house and so she had nowhere to go, no comfort of a bed to sleep in, no clothes, no personal needs, just locked out, dropped, damaged, rejected, unloved once again by the man who said he loved her. By a man who declared he was a Christian.

The question here is, Is that what Christian men are supposed to do? I am sure that we Christians should follow the example of Jesus and that is to love, not to harm or hurt anyone.

Oh, what was she to do now? How could she stop the disaster that was about to happen?

"Don't let what you thought you were yesterday keep you from becoming what you're meant to be today."

— Vironika Tugaleva

"Seek God every morning.

Trust God every moment."

— Lailah Gifty Akita

Chapter 9.

The beginning of the end

After one anger session, Mary went to the doctor, as she tried to hide the bruises, but she knew she could not go to work looking like that. The doctor asked if she was safe in the house, but Mary said all was okay. But that was not true. Mary was frightened, very frightened, but she wanted to keep her marriage. She did not want to fail God or herself.

Mary kept praying and calling out to God. She had close friends doing the same. All Mary wanted was for the beating, the anger and the violence and abuse to stop and that her marriage would become what God had ordained marriage to be.

As her husband had become unemployed, Mary gave him a position at the kindergarten, but he started to deal inappropriately with children and so Mary had to dismiss him after he had been given many chances. That's when this man's plan to destroy Mary came to light.

All this time, Mary was having counselling from a professional who repeatedly told her she should not stay in the midst of this violence and abuse. But Mary wanted her marriage to work, as she was convinced that God had brought them together.

How wrong could she be? She meditated on this many times. Mary called on God for comfort and the Lord spoke to her, saying:

"I the Lord gave you both a chance, a test, and your husband failed it. Mary, you are now a widow."

Mary was amazed at God's word to her, but she knew He had spoken to her. *"I have a plan for your life, Mary, I want only good for you. And I will never leave you or forsake you,"* said the Lord. Mary was thankful that she belonged to the one and only living God.

Mary tried to keep up appearances, but the beatings just got worse till she feared for her life. This man was very sick and out of control all the time and Mary was walking on "eggshells" to try and keep the peace and not get battered and broken.

At this time, Mary was the senior pastor of a local church and Mary told the church board all that was going on and that she said she would step down from her position. But the board said no, that the vision for the church was from God through Mary, so she remained as the senior pastor. The board stated that it was not her fault and God would not want Mary to step down from her position.

JAMES 1: 13 – 15 "LET NO ONE SAY HE IS TEMPTED, TEMPT BY GOD, FOR GOD CAN NOT BE TEMPTED BY EVIL NOR DOES HE HIMSELF TEMPT BY ANYONE. BUT EACH ONE IS TEMPTED WHEN HE IS DRAWN AWAY BY HIS OWN DESIRES AND ENTICED. THEN WHEN DESIRE HAS CONCEIVED IT GIVES BIRTH TO SIN AND SIN WHEN IT IS FULL GROWN BRINGS FORTH DEATH."

God purifies each one of us unto holy living.

JAMES 2: 13 SAYS, "FOR JUDGEMENT IS WITHOUT MERCY TO THE ONE WHO HAS SHOWN NO MERCY." MERCY TRIUMPHS OVER JUDGEMENT. VERSE 26 SAYS "FOR AS THE BODY WITHOUT THE SPIRIT IS DEAD, SO FAITH WITHOUT WORKS IS DEAD ALSO.

"To reach your goals you've got to get rid of your butt. A butt is nothing more than a Barrier Undermining The Truth! The truth is you are more powerful than you realize."

—— Rodney Walker

Chapter 10.

Ashes to beauty

B ut all this abuse had not brought Mary down. She is stronger now than ever before because God has helped her and given her a new vision for her life. God said to Mary:

"SOMETHING BEAUTIFUL, SOMETHING GOOD, ALL YOUR CONFUSION I UNDERSTOOD, ALL YOU HAD TO OFFER ME WAS BROKENESS AND STRIFE. NOW I WILL MAKE SOMETHING BEAUTIFUL OF YOUR LIFE."

That's what God did for Mary: He made something beautiful of her life. Yes, Mary was forgiven, just like the woman at the well. Just look at what God has done in Mary's life and I know He will do the same for you.

She was a broken woman: battered, and destroyed physically and mentally. Her heart was broken, and God mended this broken heart. God loves Mary and has chosen her to preach the gospel of love, the gospel of Jesus Christ to all mankind.

Mary did not trust anyone. *What will they do to me?* she thought. *How would they hurt me?* she voiced many times. Mary vowed never to let anyone hurt her again. At one time, Mary hardened her heart, but Jesus softened it again.

Guilt was rampant in Mary's mind. She would do almost anything so that her husband would like her and give her his approval and acceptance. Love unconditionally is all Mary wanted, but all was in vain.

Many people today feel the same way. They have been hurt, abused and rejected just like Mary. These people will suffer from guilt feelings and then they will seek approval from others to try and forget the pain. When you seek another person's approval, it can become an addiction and it can control you if you don't recognise it. The biggest hurdle in Mary's life was accepting herself, forgiving herself and looking at herself as a failure.

For we are all made in the image and likeness of God. If only we all could recognise this and accept ourselves as God made us: in His image and likeness.

God did not reject Mary. Mary rejected herself and some Christians reject other Christians and judge them. We all make many mistakes; we all make bad choices at times, and Mary believed that she was bad, ugly, uneducated, the scum of the earth and that no one would want her as their treasure.

But God renewed her mind. He showed her she was beautiful. In fact, He told her she was His special rose and that she had a beautiful perfume, the Lord's perfume.

Mary was abused by her parents for 15 plus years and by her husband who left her for another woman. She had to have a hysterectomy at aged 31 years due to a disease. She suffered with anxiety and had electric shock treatment. Her friends deserted her, lied to her, stole from her and talked about her with lies and exaggeration and in ungodly ways. She was judged, ridiculed, rejected, dropped and unwanted and unloved by the people who said they loved her. Some were supposed to be Christians.

But God never left her He was always there for her. God was and is faithful to Mary and she is still here on this earth working for the Lord in what He has called her to do.

Now many of you have been in the same boat as Mary. Many of you have gone through the same abuse as Mary, but some of you have allowed these circumstances to cause you to make ungodly and bad choices. Don't let that happen again. Remember that God will never leave you or forsake you. He is always there for us to call on, and remember, He wants us to have life and life abundantly with His grace and his joy.

Many people have had a bad experience of life as a child and many people have insecurities because of their past which influenced their life choices. Mary too had many problems and for a while she let them make her choices, and they were bad choices. She felt bad about her life, about herself. It was stealing her joy and damaging her relationships with other people.

Mary needed to celebrate the good things in her life and forget the not so good things. Then joy comes in to our lives and we want to celebrate. We all have special occasions in our lives that we celebrate, but the best celebration should be when God saved us from destruction. If we remember the miracles God has done for us in the past, we would not result to worry, fear and the feeling of rejection, for the truth always stands and the lies fade away and the truth will set us free.

"God knows our situation; He will not judge us as if we had no difficulties to overcome. What matters is the sincerity and perseverance of our will to overcome them."

— C.S. Lewis

Chapter 11.

Love is The answer.

L ove is the answer, but many people do not know how to love, or they
choose not to love out of selfishness. If you don't ever love, you will
end up with emotional pain, feeling rejected and unwanted. Then you
end up not approving of yourself and not forgiving yourself. People who
reject and hate themselves and do not love are on the road to failure and
a life of misery. Love can start with forgiveness.

It says in God's word,

CORINTHIANS 13: 4: "LOVE SUFFERS LONG AND IS KIND, DOES
NOR ENVY, LOVE DOES NOT PARADE ITSELF, IS NOT PUFFED UP."

And in,

1 CORINTHIANS 13:13 "AND NOW ABIDE FAITH HOPE
LOVE THESE THREE BUT THE GREATEST IS LOVE."

God will give us favour if we ask Him and we put our trust in Him. *We
just have to repent.*

PROVERBS 16:7 SAYS: "WHEN A MAN'S WAYS PLEASE THE LORD
HE MAKES EVEN HIS ENEMIES TO BE AT PEACE WITH HIM."

Let me tell you, it's not easy to get through abuse, and many people do not understand the emotion that goes with it and they judge harshly.

Many Christians judge other Christians, not allowing them to be accepted after repentance. No matter where you have been or what you have done, God forgives.

It is time for Christians to forgive each other's pasts and walk in love with that person who was broken, dropped, rejected and abused. God's grace is for all mankind not just a few, but for all. Even the lost, the lonely, the hurting, the rejected… God's grace is for all. God loves all mankind. He made them in His image and likeness.

Even friends of an abused person are judgemental at times. They say, "Why didn't you run away?" They have no idea the power that an abuser has over the victim and so they judge. But to get through that emotion, where the victim of the person who is judging needs forgiveness, because one day they will have to learn to forgive themselves when they come to know the truth. Because when we know the truth, the truth will set us free.

1 JOHN 4:7 SAYS: "BRETHREN, LET US LOVE
ONE ANOTHER FOR LOVE IS OF GOD."

As you have read earlier, Mary was raised in a very dysfunctional family. It was a home filled with violence, abuse, anger and fear and because of this abuse, she felt unacceptable. She was ashamed of her life. She did not like herself, and so when she met different people, she felt not good enough. She felt she was ugly, stupid and the scum of the earth and not good enough to be alive.

Poor Mary. She only ever thought bad and negative things about herself. What did the nuns say to Mary? She was bad, through and through. What did her mother tell her? She was not wanted. This innocent little girl was unloved and rejected by everyone: her family, her friends and anyone that knew about her past.

If you are reading this book, I want to ask you a question. How did Jesus act while He was on this earth?

Did Jesus reject anyone or abuse anyone? No. He protected them and built them up, especially those who were hurting, rejected and unloved. Shouldn't we be doing the same?

Before Mary met Jesus, she believed that she was not worthy of anything good in her life, especially a husband. Mary would always expect to be abused and beaten if someone said they loved her. She had no confidence in herself, but would act as if she had. She looked strong and in control, but she wasn't. And because she expected nothing great or good in her life, that is what she got: nothing good... Until she met Jesus.

Jesus is the answer. Jesus is love. so love is the answer.

Until God intervened and changed her outlook in life, Mary had nothing to look forward to and had no idea what love was. Then God showed her what love really was and He can show you what love is, if you don't know. For He died on the cross just for each one of us and the Father rose Him from the dead and He is now seated at the right hand of the Father.

Personally I can't wait to see my Lord in heaven.

God gave Mary the strength to stand up and be counted as a strong woman, but let me tell you, the devil has tried to ruin her time and time again through other people. They rejected her, lied about her, gossiped about her, judged her, stole from her and these were Christian people that said they loved her.

These people allowed Satan to use them to try to destroy Mary, but God had His way and she survived. Mary came out on top because that is what God wanted. Praise God.

God wants us to expect good and great things from Him, not bad things. He has many good gifts for each one of us, and God will give us His favour, if we ask and expect it. Satan will give us rejection and disapproval if we let him, so expect the best and the best will come.

We all make mistakes, but mistakes are there for our growth. We can either look at a mistake as a failure, or learn from it. God wants us to learn and then He will give us what we desire.

Many times through our mistakes we feel hopeless, worthless, dirty and ugly by the circumstances and the choices we have made. But dirty or clean, we are still precious to our Father in heaven. Repent and we are forgiven and our sins are thrown into the sea of forgetfulness. And once again, we can be of value to our community. Did you know that God chose the foolish people in the world to put the wise to shame and the weak to put the strong to shame?

1 CORINTHIANS 1 : 27: "FOR GOD HAS CHOSEN THE FOOLISH THINGS OF THE WORLD TO PUT TO SHAME THE WISE, AND GOD HAS CHOSEN THE WEAK THINGS OF THE WORLD TO PUT TO SHAME THE THINGS WHICH ARE MIGHTY."

Satan is out to deceive and destroy us, especially when we have made a mistake. He will put guilt and shame on us, but we must be strong and stand firm on the word of God. It says in God's word to resist the devil and he will flee. We must say, "Get behind me, Satan, in the name of Jesus Christ," and he has to go.

JAMES 4: 7 "THEREFORE SUBMIT TO GOD AND HE WILL FLEE FROM YOU. DRAW NEAR TO GOD AND HE WILL DRAW NEAR TO YOU."

Love is the answer. Jesus is the answer, for He is love.

Satan uses our feeling of rejection to deceive us, but once we see and hear the truth, the truth will set us free. Remember, rejection can be a door to destruction and Satan loves us to feel rejection, as this can then cause us to reject others, causing even more problems in our lives. But love and forgiveness are the answer.

It's not an easy road at times, but if we have Jesus in our hearts, love and forgiveness is an easy path to travel. The Holy Spirit, if we ask Him, will come and make His home in our hearts and life will become much easier as we give our will over to His will. THY WILL BE DONE NOT MY WILL LORD.

When you live in a world of abuse you think it is normal, but you don't like it or want it. You live in secret. No one must know. So you carry the secret for years, which becomes a burden, until one day you blurt it out, then your family rejects you, saying you are lying and you are never allowed to be part of the family again. Another rejection.

It's then you start to think that you are bad and it's all your fault. Then the guilt comes, and more guilt, more shame, till you want to die. But it is then you call on the name of Jesus and He tells you how much He loves you. He will never reject you. He will always love you.

It can be a vicious circle, but trust in God and wait for His miracles.

I too have felt rejected from an early age and it took me many years to know and feel that God loves me and will never reject me. When I realised this, my life changed. My life choices started to become great and I continued to make good choices. And rejection was gone from my thoughts. Praise God. Mary also went through this same process, same feelings, and God brought her through. He will do the same for you if you ask.

You see, God loves us so much that He sent His only begotten Son to die on the cross for us all. When you feel this way as I do, then you know you are loved by God for who you are, for who God made you to be. He made us in His image and likeness…

Mary has now got to the point that she knows she is loved by God, the King of Kings, and is now the King's Daughter.

"You deserve to be healthy, wealthy and loved. You deserve to achieve the level of material success that is important to you. You deserve to be respected and admired at home, at work and in your community and you deserve to wake up each day at peace with yourself and with your world. You deserve it all!"

—— Max Patrick

Chapter 12.

Mary's dreams and desires.

Mary's desire has always been to be loved and cherished by a man on this earth. To have a husband, a best friend, a person who she can share anything with, someone who wants her for who she is, someone who loves the Lord and wants to follow in His ways. If that does not happen, then its God's will and Mary is at peace, for she only wants God's will in her life.

Yes, this is the true story of Mary Maddison, and with her approval, I have written down all she has told me. She has been to hell and now to heaven on this earth. She has the ability to minister to others because of her past because God has called her to do so.

Mary's father stole her childhood. He violated her physically and mentally, which scared her for many years. In the past, she seemed to accept only those men that were abusive and angry because she thought she was not good enough to be loved for who she was, only to be abused. That's what Mary thought love was for many years: just abuse.

Look what God has done for Mary. He made her His daughter, He chose her to be the daughter of the King, The Great I Am, the Lover of our souls and the Lifter of our heads.

So, my friend, when you meet a victim of abuse, accept her, love her and help her through this time of renewing. For this woman who has been broken, dropped, damaged beaten and almost destroyed, but now healed by the almighty Father, is the daughter of the King, from ashes to beauty, to the King's daughter.

Conclusion.

There are many women in our neighbourhood today that are and have gone through a similar childhood and they need help, they need the love of Jesus, they need our love. Why not show them the love that's in your hearts and be Jesus to them? Christ is calling us to be like Him and this is one way we can help the lost, the lonely, the abused and the neglected, the rejected, the unloved in this world, especially in our own community. Love like Jesus loves, unconditionally.

Maybe you are facing a disaster yourself: a problem a bad choice, an illness, financial issue, a divorce, a family member dying, children causing worry right now and there seems no way out or no way forward. You are just desperate for the situation to get better.

The truth is it does not matter what the issue or problem is, nothing is impossible for God. All things are possible for Him. Just take time out to seek His face, read His word, call on the name of Jesus, and tell Him your problem and invite Him into your life. Whether it is the first, second or tenth time, just invite Him in again and see what miracles He performs just for you.

Like the woman at the well, God has forgiven each and every one of us and wants only good for us. He loves us all unconditionally. He loves you so much and wants only good for you, so seek Him today make Him your Lord and see the difference He will make of your life.

God does not care where you have been, what you have done, who you have associated with or slept with. He is not counting your sins. All He wants is for you to love Him and give Him your heart, as He loves you.

Remember, He will never leave you of forsake you, He is always there, waiting for you to respond to His call.

If you have never given your heart to Jesus, well now is your opportunity. Tell him you are sorry for your sins and want Him to be your savour from this day forward and He will respond to your call.

Mary Maddison is a woman, aged 73 years who was broken, beaten, dropped, rejected, unloved and almost destroyed by men who said they loved her. Well, she is now born again of God. He brought her from ashes to beauty, He made her the daughter of the King of Kings.

She is The King's Daughter and He is so proud of her. She has come through many abusive ordeals, but after she met Jesus, she never looked back. She is truly The King's Daughter.

What else could any woman wish for? The Lord is our strength and He has made us to be His daughters. We are the King's daughters, so don't forget it.

This story does not end here. It's just the beginning. So much more happiness and love is about to come into Mary's life and God made it happen. Now the King reigns in Mary's life, she is truly The King's Daughter.

As I listened to Mary and wrote this book, I would like to add my thoughts to anyone who has trials and tribulations, anyone who is or has been abused, dropped, broken or rejected. Listen carefully.

You are not your past, for in Christ we are a new creation. The past is behind you and today and the future is before you. Make this life special for the glory of God. Don't look back; don't dwell on the past. The woman at the well put her past behind her and focused on the future with Christ Jesus. She became the woman that she was born to be: the first woman evangelist.

Today is a new day and the past is gone. Rejoice in the Lord, for He is your strength. He is your comfort and He is the one who knows every hair on your head. He has carved you in the palm of His hand.

So look to the future, for you can't change the past, but you can change your future. The choice is yours.

To be with Christ or not to be with Christ, that's your decision. Mary chose Christ, and look how her life changed. She became The King's Daughter.

"I think that little by little I'll be able
to solve my problems and survive."

—— Frida Kahlo

"Be grateful for the tests, difficulties and challenges
you are going through, because it's preparing you
for the Next Level and your Breakthrough."

—— Jeanette Coron

Chapter 13.

The Prayer

If you want to commit your life to Jesus and you don't know what to say, here is a simple prayer for you to say and believe it.

Dear God, I know that I am a sinner; I know that You love me and want to give me eternal life. Jesus, I believe in You. I believe You are the Son of God, who died on the cross for my sins. I believe that God raised You from the dead and You are now sitting at the right hand of the Father. I now, by faith, open my heart and receive you as my personal Saviour and Lord. Come into my heart and forgive me my sins. Show me your ways, and bring me to a place of rest in You. Open my heart Lord, I want to see Jesus. Open my ears Lord, I want to hear Jesus.

I pray this in the name of Jesus. Amen.

ACTS 9:15. (SPIRIT FILLED KING JAMES BIBLE),
"GO YOUR WAY FOR YOU ARE A CHOSEN VESSEL UNTO ME TO BEAR MY
NAME AMONG THE PEOPLE. FOR I WILL SHOW YOU GREAT THINGS
AND YOU WILL SUFFER FOR MY NAMES SAKE SAYS THE LORD."

"Nothing is better for self-esteem than survival."

—— Martha Getthorn

"Encouragers turn mountains into molehills.
Discouragers turn molehills into mountains."

—— Cathy Burnham Martin

From The Author

And I Carolann Kelleher have also become "THE KINGS DAUGHTER". He has filled my life with the richness of love, given me back what the evil one took away. He has taken away my shame, my guilt and my sins. He has showered me with blessings and favour, and I will always be most grateful to the King of Kings. He has honoured me as His daughter and in the world, He has given me respect. All because I made myself available to Him and I had the desire to change from ashes to beauty. Praise God.

A personal word that God gave me, Carolann, on the 1st January 2018. The Lord said:

ISAIAH 54: 4 (SPIRIT FILLED KING JAMES BIBLE),

"DO NOT FEAR, CAROLANN, FOR YOU WILL NOT BE ASHAMED. NEITHER BE DISGRACED OR DEPRESSED, FOR YOU WILL NOT BE PUT TO SHAME. FOR YOU SHALL FORGET THE SHAME OF YOUR YOUTH AND YOU WILL NOT REMEMBER THE REPROACH OF YOUR WIDOWHOOD ANYMORE."

On the 9th of December 2018 God spoke to me, Carolann, saying,

"SEE HOW *I* CHANGED THE LIFE OF THE WOMAN WHOSE HUSBAND DIED AND LEFT HER IN DEBT AND HER SONS WERE TO GO INTO SLAVERY TO PAY HER DEBTS. GOD FILLED HER URNS WITH OIL TO OVERFLOWING (WHICH WAS AT THAT TIME MORE PRECIOUS THAN GOLD) AND SHE WAS ABLE TO PAY HER DEBTS. THIS WOMAN OBEYED ME SAID THE LORD AND *I* REPAID HER WITH A MIRACLE. *I* WILL DO THE SAME FOR YOU CAROLANN. JUST TRUST ME. IT WILL COME TO PASS, *I* THE LORD WILL FULFIL MY PROMISE TO YOU."

"The Gospels are full of testimonies of God's power from eyewitnesses who saw Jesus heal the sick and raise the dead. When the blind man received sight, he went and told others. When the Samaritan woman received living water from Jesus, she went back to tell what happened to her, and 'many of the Samaritans from that town believed in Him because of the woman's testimony" (John 4:39). Revelation 12:11 says we overcome the evil one by the word of our testimony. When the orphans tell, they experience God's power at work in them; when others hear, their faith is strengthened. When we gather to share our stories, I know the devil runs out the door when the smallest, weakest orphan stands up to attest to the goodness of God. (p178)"

—— Eric Irivuzumugabe

www.ingramcontent.com/pod-product-compliance
Lightning Source LLC
LaVergne TN
LVHW051422080426
835508LV00022B/3200